This book belongs to:

Cosima-i.-C.

From

Funded in part by the D.C. Commission on the Arts & Humanities, an agency supported in part by the National Endowment for the Arts

www.anopenbookfound.org

Copyright © 2024 by Carrie Maslen
Published by Stirred Stories.

All rights reserved.

No part of this publication may be reproduced, distributed, or transmitted in any form or by any means, including photocopying, recording, or other electronic or mechanical methods, without the prior written permission of the publisher, except as permitted by U.S. copyright law. For permission requests, contact hello@stirredstories.com.

First edition: May 2024

ATTENTION SCHOOLS AND BUSINESSES:
Stirred Stories books are available at a discount for bulk purchase. For more information, please email hello@stirredstories.com.

Baking Bread with Jiddo

Written and Illustrated by
Carrie Maslen

Carrie Maslen

Carrie Waller

To Paige, Andrew, and Zoe

Every summer, we pack the car and drive for two days to visit Jiddo.

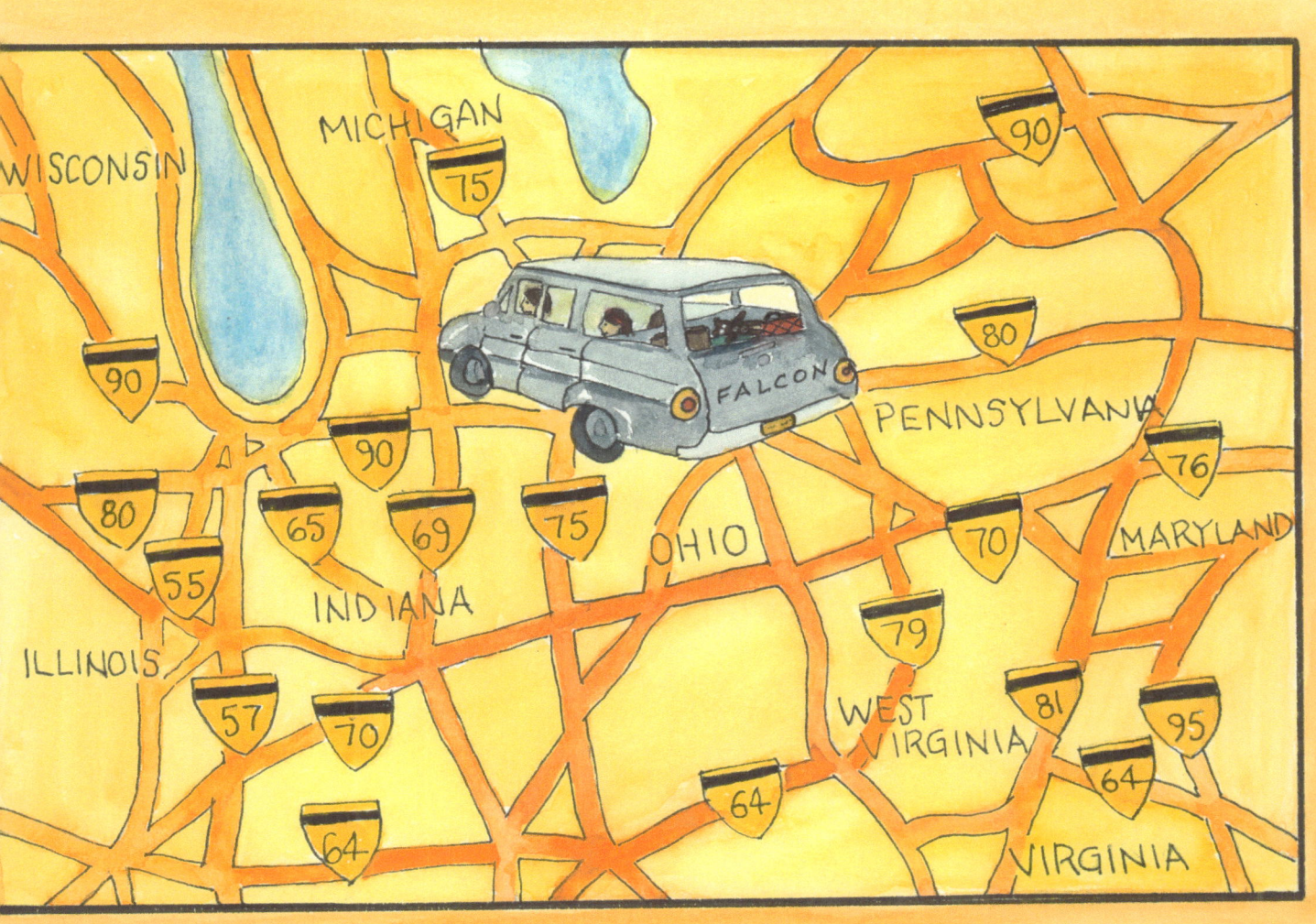

We pull up to his yellow house with a squeaky swing on the front porch.

Jiddo greets us with open arms and a happy smile that makes his eyes crinkle.

In his basement, there's a shower with a flowered curtain, a creaky washing machine, and an ancient oven on the back wall.

until Jiddo pulls the string to turn on the light.
That's when it becomes my favorite place.

In the morning,
while everyone is still asleep,
I follow the cozy smell and
tiptoe down the stairs.

"You remembered," Jiddo smiles as he hugs me.

"Of course," I grin. "I'm your helper!"

I knead the dough with him.

When it sticks to my fingers, Jiddo sprinkles flour on my hands.

"Don't be shy with the flour," he says.

I pat the pillows of dough into round loaves with him, and we send puffs of flour everywhere.

"Pat from the edges," he says. "That turns them into circles."

I put the bread in the oven with him and take it out with his charred paddle.

Then it's time to taste the first loaf. Will it be crispy and crunchy?

"Scrumptious!" I announce.

"Tayeb," Jiddo agrees.
"That's Arabic for delicious."

I take another bite.
"Tell me a story, Jiddo."

And he tells me a few about when he was a young boy in Lebanon:

A story about picking juicy peaches for breakfast,

about tickling his toes in the cool village stream,

about sailing to America with his mother and older brother and searching for his father at the dock.

One morning, I wake up suddenly.

I sit up in bed, but I don't smell the warm yeast.

I walk down the hall, but I don't see the soft glow of the basement light.

I listen, but I don't hear the oven door open and shut.

Something is wrong.

"ACHOO!"

"Jiddo," I call as I rush into his bedroom. "Are you okay?"

"Just a bad cold," he says. "You'll have to be the baker today."

"Me?" I ask. "I don't know how!"

"You know. You're my helper."

"But I don't know how to make the dough!"

"I made the dough last night."

"But my loaves are never round like yours!"

"The shape doesn't matter."

Jiddo draws up his blue blanket.

"But I can't even reach the string to turn on the light!"

"You can do it," Jiddo murmurs, as he closes his eyes.

"Now go, or we won't have bread today."

I peek into the dark basement and take a brave breath.

I plod down the basement steps and try to turn on the light but I can't reach the string.

What can I do?

I search in the darkness, spot a stool, and drag it over to reach the light.

The basement feels empty without Jiddo.

I try to remember where to start.

I separate the dough into balls and cover them with the red and white checkered towel.

I drop two, but I pick them up quickly, dust them off, and they're as good as new.

By the time I've made the last mound, it's time to start patting.

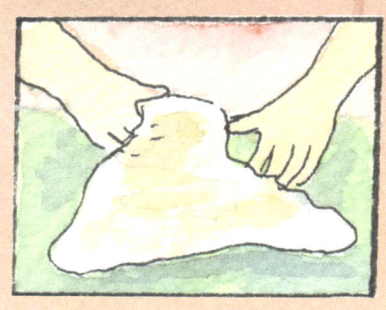  

The first one sticks to the counter and jiggles into a jumble of dough.

Then I remember:
"Don't be shy with the flour!"

No matter how hard I try, it won't go into a circle.

Then I remember: "Pat from the edges!"

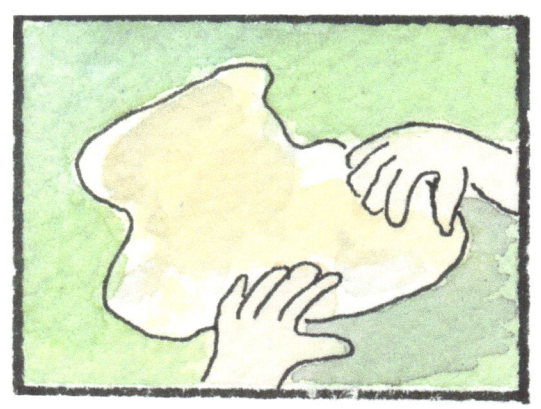

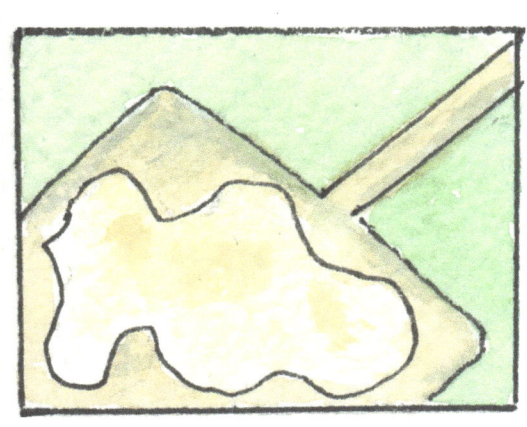

I put the first loaf onto the paddle, and open the oven door.

I forgot to turn on the oven!

That's OK.
I know how to do that.

I sit down to wait.

DING!

I open the oven door,
slide in the first loaf.

Brown smoke seeps out of the oven.
Oh no—that was too long!

The second loaf only burns a little on the top.

Still too long.

I don't burn the third loaf, or any of the others.

I stack each steaming loaf as it comes out of the oven just like Jiddo does.

I carry them up to the kitchen, put a few of the loaves on a tray, and take them upstairs to Jiddo's bedroom.

"Time to taste the first loaf," I announce.

"It smells wonderful," Jiddo smiles.

But will it be crispy and crunchy?

"Delectable," Jiddo announces,
as he takes another bite.

"Tayeb!" I agree.

And as we eat, Jiddo tells more stories:

About meeting my grandmother, about opening his grocery store, about baking his first loaf of bread.

"A little burned," he sighs, "but I learned."

As we talk, the rest of the family trickles into his room.

And Jiddo tells a new story about a new baker.

Author's Note

As a child, I looked forward to our summer visits to see my grandfather. I loved watching him work at his basement oven. Once he rolled up his sleeves and put on his white apron, he was ready to bake. I can still remember waking up to the smell of his fresh dough, unwrapping the tea towel to see the neat stack of bread, and slathering my very own warm and crunchy loaf with butter.

My grandfather was 11 when he emigrated from Lebanon to the United States with his mother and older brother. He was one of 605,000 immigrants who arrived at Ellis Island in New York in 1912.

His father had come to the United States seven years earlier and had finally saved enough money to bring his wife and children to his new country.

Although the trip to Ellis Island was seven days, it was a world apart from the village my grandfather left. When he sailed to America, Lebanon was not yet an independent country. It was in an area of the Ottoman Empire called Greater Syria. His first home in the United States was a tenement house at 13 Washington Street, in a neighborhood of New York City called Little Syria, even though people from dozens of countries lived there at the time.

In New York, he saw tall buildings instead of mountains, explored streets and sidewalks instead of farmland and terraces, smelled crowded tenements instead of fresh streams, and heard people speaking many languages. I can only imagine his sense of wonder about the new life awaiting him.

My grandfather eventually settled in Wisconsin, where he opened a grocery store, Tom's Fruit Market, to support his family. He welcomed relatives, friends, and new immigrants to his home where they shared stories, songs, and Lebanese suppers—always with fresh bread. He and my grandmother raised five children, one of whom was my father.

He didn't learn how to bake until his wife died, when he was almost 60 years old. I never met my grandmother, but her first name is my middle name.

My grandfather left Lebanon for the same reasons many others have left their homelands: To seek freedom, safety, stability, equality, a better life, and to join their families.

Because of instability and unrest in Lebanon and in many other places around the world, people continue to leave their home countries in search of opportunity. They bring their traditions and recipes with them, and share them with new neighbors, new communities, and new generations of their family.

Jiddo's Middle Eastern Bread Recipe

Traditional bread in Lebanon and the Middle East is flat and round, rather than tall and rectangular like a lot of bread in a grocery store. You can use this recipe to bake loaves in any size, shape, or thickness you want. I like to bake loaves about an inch thick, called *talami* (ta-LAH-me).

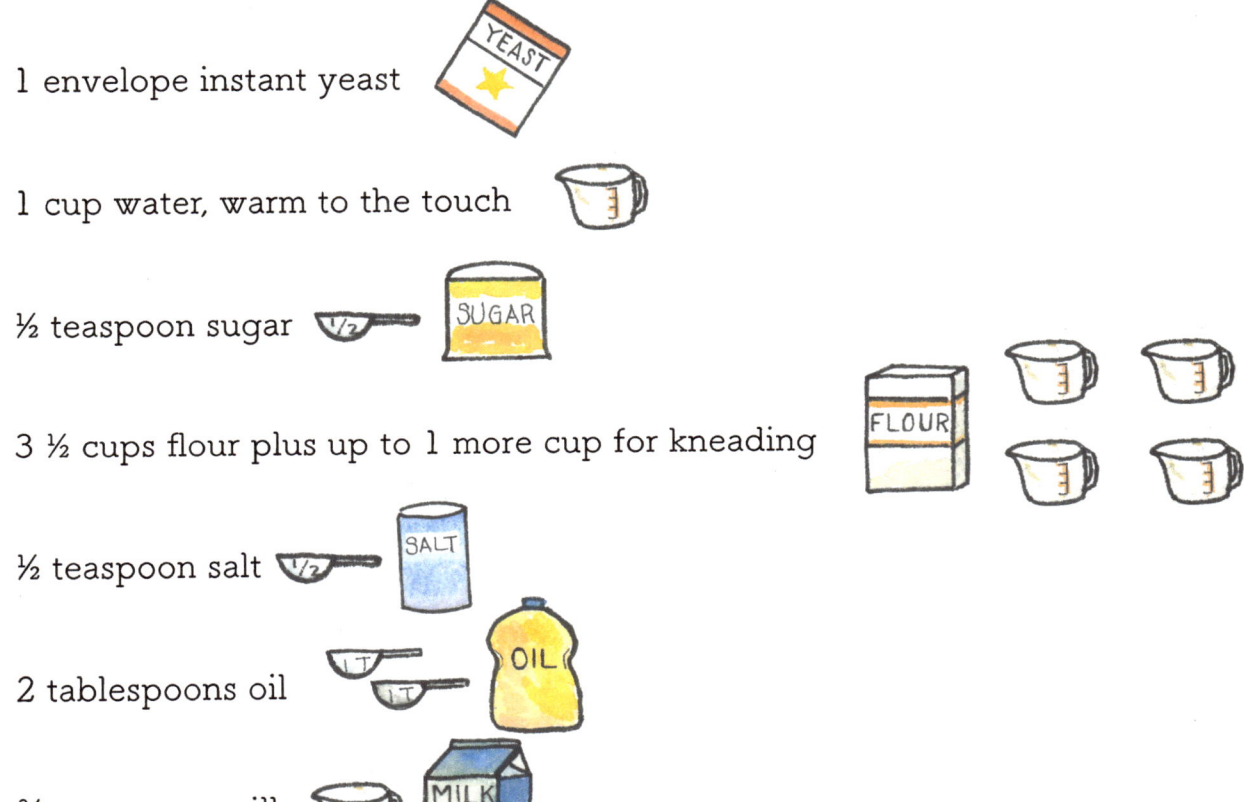

1 envelope instant yeast

1 cup water, warm to the touch

½ teaspoon sugar

3 ½ cups flour plus up to 1 more cup for kneading

½ teaspoon salt

2 tablespoons oil

¾ cup warm milk

Combine yeast, sugar, and water in a large bowl. It should be foamy in 1-2 minutes.
Add the flour, salt, oil, and milk to the yeast mixture. Stir until it comes together.
Knead the dough in the bowl, and add more flour (¼ cup at a time) until the dough comes together in a ball and becomes smooth.
Cover the bowl with a towel, and let it rest for 1-2 hours, until the dough has doubled.
Divide the dough into 2 or 3 parts, and pat each piece of dough on a floured surface into a circle about ½ inch thick, and then move it to a lightly oiled baking sheet.
Cover with a clean towel, and let it rest anywhere from 15 minutes to an hour or more. Pat it out a little more until it's the size you want it.
Bake at 425 for about 20 minutes. It's done when it's golden brown on the top and bottom, and sounds hollow when you tap it. You might have to move it to the lowest rack to brown the bottom.

About Stirred Stories

The same stories have repeatedly been told.
We're here to stir that up.

We believe that in order to create a truly just society, the stories we consume must be diverse and equitable. That's why we center authenticity and diversity in everything we do, from the books we publish to how we publish them. In short, we're *publishing for a better tomorrow.*

Follow along with us at www.stirredstories.com.

Carrie Maslen has been writing and drawing since elementary school, which is also when her family started making their two-day drive to Wisconsin where she watched her grandfather bake Arabic bread. In addition to writing for her children and grandchildren, she also wrote business material throughout her career in high tech. When she's not writing, you can find Carrie reading, cooking, gardening, and spending time with her family.

Printed in the USA
CPSIA information can be obtained
at www.ICGtesting.com
LVHW070357301024
795160LV00003B/11